D1486603

War in the Gulf

OPERATION DESERT SHIELD

Written By: Paul J. Deegan

Published by Abdo & Daughters, 6535 Cecilia Circle, Edina, Minnesota 55439.

Library bound edition distributed by Rockbottom Books, Pentagon Tower, P.O. Box 36036, Minneapolis, Minnesota 55435.

Library of Congress Number: 91-073079   ISBN: 1-56239-022-8

Cover Photo by: Bettmann
Inside Photos by: Reuters/Bettmann: 6, 10, 19, 25, 26, 27, 29, 31, 32, 34, 35
                          UPI/Bettmann: 20

Edited by: Rosemary Wallner

TABLE OF CONTENTS

THE INVASION

In the late summer of 1990, Iraq had massed about 100,000 troops on its border with the small, oil-rich country of Kuwait. Iraq's President Saddam Hussein had been quarreling with Kuwait since mid-summer. He accused Kuwait of driving down oil prices. Despite the movement of Iraqi troops to the border, the United States and other nations thought Saddam was bluffing.

He wasn't. Before dawn on August 2, Saddam ordered his tanks and infantry to move into Kuwait. The Kuwaitis fought back. But the Kuwaiti army numbered only 20,000. Their resistance was brief. Sheikh Jaber al Ahmad al Sabah was the emir of Kuwait, fled by helicopter from the presidental palace. Kuwait's ruler took refuge in Saudi Arabia.

United States President George Bush called Iraq's action "naked aggression." Right away, he ordered a ban on most trade with Iraq. He also froze Iraq's and Kuwait's assets in the United States. And he sent a U.S. aircraft carrier battle group to the scene.

On August 6, 1990, President Bush ordered U.S. forces to Saudi Arabia. White House Press Secretary Marlin Fitzwater said "Operation Desert Shield" was underway. Military men and women would be sent halfway around the world. They would be based in Saudi Arabia, which borders both Kuwait and Iraq.

Two-and-one-half months later, Operation Desert Shield was full blown. The United States had committed over 475,000 troops to a theater of war in southwest Asia. U.S. troops in Saudi Arabia and the adjoining Persian Gulf included men and women from the Army, Navy, Air Force, Marines, and Coast Guard. It would become the largest U.S. military buildup since the Vietnam War.

The U.S Military buildup in the Persian Gulf was no easy task.

U.S. TROOPS COMMITTED

Operation Desert Shield was to be the first step in liberating Kuwait. President Bush said he was going to "draw a line in the sand." It was a line Saddam Hussein should not cross. The message to Saddam was that the United States would view an attack on Saudi Arabia as an attack on itself.

Within days, such an attack would also be an attack on American forces. The first troops sent under the Operation Desert Shield label left for Saudi Arabia on August 7. They included 2,300 paratroopers. F-15 fighter planes, F-111 fighter-bombers, B-52 bombers, and AWACS radar planes were also on their way to the gulf. So were two more carrier groups.

Hundreds of thousands of American troops followed. National Guard and Reserve units were called up. Some went to the gulf. Others replaced regular-service troops sent to Saudi Arabia.

THE SAUDI CONNECTION

Saudi Arabia is the only country other than Iraq that borders Kuwait. Saudi Arabia also has a 425-mile northern border with Iraq. Saudi Arabia was where a military force to oppose Iraq had to be stationed to be the most effective.

Also, President Bush feared that Iraq might move from Kuwait into Saudi Arabia. The desert kingdom's oil riches are even greater than those of Kuwait and Iraq. If Iraq also occupied the Saudi kingdom, it would control nearly one-half of the world's known oil reserves.

President Bush wanted to place U.S. troops in Saudi Arabia to prevent Saddam from moving farther south, but it was not certain at first if Saudi Arabia would welcome a largely Western military force within its borders. Saudi Arabia was a nation withdrawn from the world. The ruling house of Saud kept a tight rein on the country. The Saudis lived in a closed society.

The Saudis were also wary of appearing too friendly with Western nations for another reason:

The Moslem holy sites of Mecca and Medina, cities of over half a million people, were both in Saudi Arabia. King Fahd ibn Abdul Aziz of Saudi Arabia feared the disapproval of other Arab nations if he allowed the presence of a large number of non-Moslem troops in Saudi Arabia. Saddam Hussein said that foreigners had been in Mecca only once. That, he said, happened 15 centuries ago.

King Fahd realized the United States would furnish the majority of the troops coming to his country. The U.S. was the major ally of Israel, an enemy of Saudi Arabia and other Arab nations. Before August 1990, there was not a single American military person in Saudi Arabia. Thus, King Fahd had "grave reservations" about seeking U.S. protection.

President Bush decided to contact the king anyway. He knew that Saddam Hussein's actions had frightened and angered the Saudis. Iraq was about to annex the Emir of Kuwait's kingdom. Iraqi troops had been lining up along Iraq's border with Saudi Arabia. King Fahd's royal army numbered only 28,000. The Saudi troops would be no match for the large Iraqi military forces.

King Fahd (right) of Saudi Arabia.

U.S. Secretary of Defense Dick Cheney flew to Saudi Arabia's capital, Riyadh (Ree-YAD). There he met with King Fahd on August 6. At the meeting, the king gave Cheney permission to place United States military forces in Saudi Arabia. The king, it was reported, "invited" U.S. troops to defend the desert kingdom.

Secretary Cheney said troops would be sent to Saudi Arabia "to deter any further Iraqi aggression." If necessary, they were "to defend Saudi Arabia against attack."

Britain hooked up to Operation Desert Shield when then-Prime Minister Margaret Thatcher honored King Fahd's request to send British air and naval troops to the gulf.

Saddam Hussein's reaction to Operation Desert Shield was to lambast the Saudis as lackeys of the West and betrayers of Islam.

ARAB NATIONS SEND TROOPS

On August 9, Egypt's President Hosni Mubarek called for an emergency meeting of the 21-nation Arab League. President Mubarek said Egypt would supply troops to a Pan-Arab force (soldiers from a union of Arab nations) to oppose Iraq. He thought that Western forces could then withdraw.

Meeting in Cairo, Egypt, the next day, the league voted to send troops to Saudi Arabia. Twelve members voted approval. Only Iraq, Libya, and the Palestine Liberation Organization voted no.

The next day troops from Egypt and Morocco arrived in Saudi Arabia. Syrian troops came three days later.

Saddam Hussein's response was to call on other Moslems to launch a "holy war" against foreign troops and "corrupt" Arab rulers.

THE UNITED NATIONS

On the day Kuwait was invaded, the United Nations (U.N.) Security Council got involved. The 15-member body voted 14-0 to condemn the Iraqi invasion. The council demanded that Iraq withdraw its troops from Kuwait.

On August 7, the Security Council voted 15-0 to declare Iraq's annexation of Kuwait "null and void."

The Bush administration returned to the Security Council several more times to gain backing for U.S. opposition to Saddam Hussein's actions. By the end of November 1990 there were 12 council resolutions relating to the gulf crisis. These included a demand for Iraq's unconditional withdrawal from Kuwait. The U.S. was in the

Persian Gulf, President Bush said repeatedly, to enforce the Security Council resolutions.

On November 29, at the urging of the United States, the Security Council set a deadline. Iraq was to withdraw from Kuwait by January 15, 1991. The measure passed 12-2 with one member not voting. If there was no withdrawal, the resolution okayed the use of military force. It said "all necessary means" could be used to force Iraq to withdraw. All the council members agreed that phrase would permit military action against Iraq.

COALITION FORMED

From the beginning, President Bush wanted to avoid the appearance of a United States-Iraq conflict. Such a matchup would have pitted perhaps the world's wealthiest nation against one of its poorest.

President Bush, armed with the first U.N. resolution, contacted many foreign leaders. He had built up relationships with foreign leaders over many years. The president wanted other nations to join the United States in establishing a military force in the Persian Gulf.

A key to the U.S. forming such a coalition was its improved relationship with the Soviet Union. The Soviets had been the major supplier of arms to Iraq. In fact, there were Soviet military advisers in Iraq when it invaded Kuwait. U.S. estimates placed the number of Soviet advisers at 500 to 1,000.

However, the Soviets immediately suspended arms sales to Iraq. A day after Iraq attacked Kuwait, there was a joint U.S.-Soviet statement. U.S. Secretary of State James Baker had been fishing in Siberia with his Soviet counterpart. The statement by Baker and Soviet Foreign Minister Eduard Shevardnadze condemned the Iraqi takeover of Kuwait.

The coalition was soon formed. Eventually, 29 nations joined the United States to form the coalition forces. By Janaury 1, 1991, there were about 300,000 troops in the gulf sent by coalition members other than the U.S.

Saudi Arabia and other Arab gulf states, including Kuwait, provided 150,000 of these troops in the Pan-Arab force okayed by the Arab League. Some 45,000 were Saudis. Egypt, which is across the Red Sea from Saudi Arabia, sent over 38,000 troops. Britain provided about 35,000 troops.

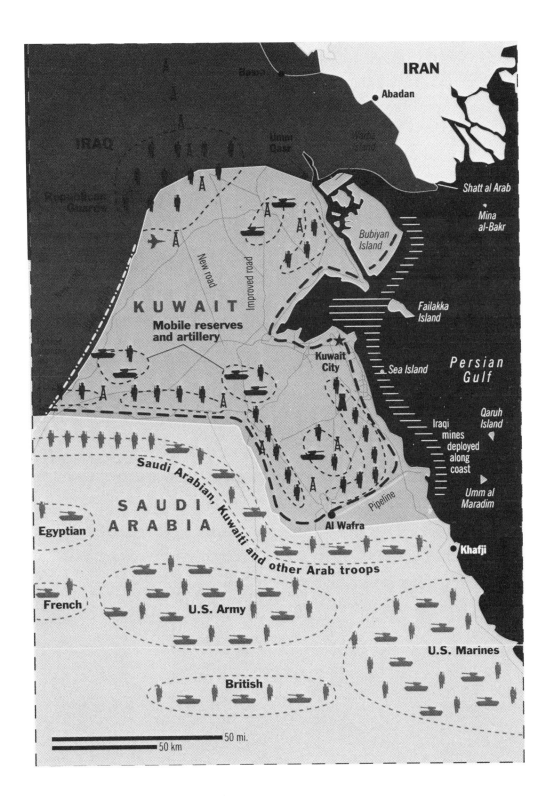

Syria sent 21,000 soldiers. Syria is northwest of Iraq. The two countries share a long border. Both Syria and Iraq are governed by a Baathist regime. Yet Syrian president Hafez Assad and Saddam Hussein are often described as "one another's archenemies." Assad had not been a U.S. favorite. However, because he was a foe of Hussein he cast his lot with the United States. President Bush declared him "rehabilitated."

The coalition forces also included over 10,000 troops from France and Pakistan.

The coalition nations were:

Argentina	Morocco
Australia	Netherlands
Bahrain	New Zealand
Bangladesh	Niger
Belgium	Norway
Britain	Oman
Canada	Pakistan
Czechoslovakia	Poland
Denmark	Quatar
Egypt	Saudi Arabia
France	Senegal
Germany	Spain
Greece	Syria
Italy	United Arab Emirates
Kuwait	United States

Eighteen other nations, including the Soviet Union and Japan, contributed economic or other assistance to the coalition. The other 16 were Afghanistan, Austria, Bulgaria, Finland, Honduras, Hungary, Iceland, Luxembourg, Malaysia, the Philippines, Portugal, Siera Leone, South Korea, Sweden, Taiwan, and Turkey.

Turkey is Iraq's northern neighbor. Like the U.S., Turkey is a member of the North Atlantic Treaty Organization. Turkey cooperated fully with the U.N. sanctions against Iraq and shut off Iraq's oil pipeline.

SCHWARZKOPF IN CHARGE

United States Army General Norman Schwarzkopf was the field commander in the region for Operation Desert Shield. H. Norman Schwarzkopf III was born in 1934. The 6-foot 3 inch, 240-pound general is known for his leadership ability — and his quick temper.

General Schwarzkopf is a student of Arab history and culture. As a young boy, he lived in Tehran, the Iranian capital. His father then worked for the U.S. government. He followed his father to West Point. He graduated in the top 10 percent of his class at the U.S. Military Academy.

In 1988 General Schwarzkopf took over U.S. Central Command for the Middle East. The most likely threat to the region's stability, he decided, was Iraq. He turned out to be correct. General Schwarzkopf ran Operation Desert Shield from an underground basement located in the Saudi Defense Ministry in Riyadh.

General Schwarzkopf reported to General Colin Powell in Washington. General Powell is the chairman of the Joint Chiefs of Staff.

Powell's superior is Secretary of Defense Dick Cheney. Cheney in turn reports to President Bush, the commander-in-chief of the United States armed forces.

Lieutenant General Khalid bin Sultan, a Saudi prince, commanded the large Arab force in the Kuwaiti theater of war.

The commanders of Desert Shield: (left to right) Chairman of the Joint Chiefs of Staff Colin Powell; Secretary of Defense Dick Cheney; and General Norman Schwarzkopf.

Female soldier prepares for the long wait during Desert Shield.

WOMEN IN THE DESERT

The American troops General Schwarzkopf commanded in Operation Desert Shield included women. The Persian Gulf conflict saw more women serving in the U.S. military than at any time in history. About 10 percent of the U.S. troops in the gulf theater were women, by one estimate. That's very close to the percentage of women in the total U.S. armed forces. About 11 percent of the two million troops are women.

The jobs held by the 30,000 women soldiers in Operation Desert Shield were more varied then ever before. Some flew giant C-141 transport planes. Others piloted Huey helicopters. Women mechanics maintained tanks. Women drove trucks.

There were women Army officers who were West Point graduates. There were women Marine military police. There were women Navy firefighters. There were women paratroopers. Women also served in various specialties such as intelligence and communications.

Federal law does not allow women to serve in combat positions in the Air Force, Marines, and Navy. The Army bans such service by policy. But the definition of "combat" has been narrowed. Thus, thousands of servicewomen in the gulf were exposed to the dangers of war.

The female troops were issued protective gear against chemical weapons. They carried arms. The women had been trained to use weapons if they needed to do so.

The American women soldiers were a culture shock to Saudi soldiers and civilians. Women do not have a primary role in Saudi society. Women officers issuing orders to men astounded the Saudis.

LIVING IN THE DESERT

Sunscreen. Lip balm. Foot powder. These were among the supplies sent with the U.S. forces stationed in Saudi Arabia.

About one-quarter the size of the United States, Saudi Arabia is a desert. The terrain is harsh. Most of the country is unpopulated.

The entire gulf region has been described as a "land so lifeless even a vulture could starve." One reporter said of the area, "It is all desert, from the Red Sea to the Persian Gulf." He said some of the desert "has buildings in it," meaning the cities and towns. An American serviceman said, "It's nothing but sand. One big beach."

When the first Western forces arrived in August, they had to adjust to daytime temperatures of over 100 degrees. There is usually no rainfall from June through September. There is humidity as well as heat from May into September. Relief comes in the summer after sunset when a cooling breeze often stirs the sand.

The troops also had to get along without many things taken for granted in the United States. There was no hot water. Tank corps troops heated water for their morning coffee on the exhausts of their tanks. Hot food was rare. The soldiers ate powdered eggs and freeze-dried meals. Drinking water came from the gulf. After it was purified, it had a foul taste. There were no soft beds and no telephones.

Hot water showers were nonexistent. One Marine said, "Heck, our smell will scare the Iraqis off if nothing else does." Enterprising soldiers rigged up cold-water showers.

There were flies, ants, beetles, spiders, poisonous snakes, and scorpions. Some scorpions were as big as mice. Some of the soldiers caught spiders and scorpions and kept them for pets.

When the U.S. soldiers first arrived in Saudi Arabia, tank corps soldiers slept on their tanks. Later, tent cities were built as the ground forces awaited a call to action. The soldiers lived in four-man tents.

During the summer heat, each soldier was advised to drink five gallons of water daily. If they were camped by an oasis, they could watch camels, goats, and wild dogs drink well water. The animals also ate dates that fell from the trees.

The men and women soldiers wrote home about the beautiful nights. "The sky comes alive with a billion stars." The moon "seems as bright as a spotlight."

By the late fall, the temperatures moderated and the desert became chilly. Early spring brings wind-driven sandstorms to the desert. They blacken the sky for miles.

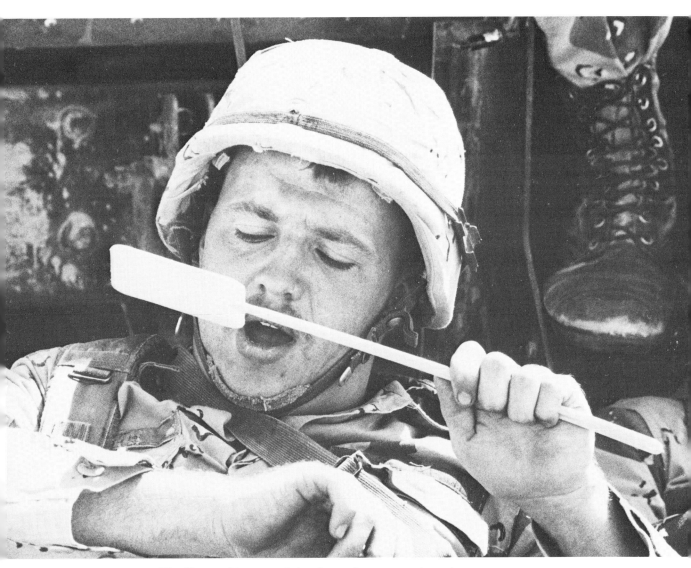

The flies and insects of the desert became a staunch enemy.

As the days turned into weeks, the weeks into months, boredom became the enemy in Operation Desert Shield. There were training missions and equipment to keep up. But recreation was limited to "Walkmans," cards, and conversation. There were no movies or television. American troops located by Saudi communities were not permitted to socialize with the Saudis.

U.S. servicemen pass the time napping as they await a call to action.

Later they usually find time to play cards.

A SCARY OPPONENT

The women and men making up the coalition forces in the gulf were facing off against the world's fourth-largest army. Iraq's overall 56-division military force was made up of 1.5 million troops. Saddam Hussein called up reserves in late August. He had 513 planes in his air force. Western military experts considered the Iraqi military machine a tough opponent.

It also was a scary one.

The allied troops, the Saudi citizens, and the residents of Israel and the West Bank worried about attacks by Iraqi Scud missiles. Israel is some 200 miles west of Iraq. This was within range of the Scuds.

The rest of the world wondered if they would be the target of terrorist attacks.

"We know that you can harm us although we do not threaten you," Saddam Hussein said to the United States. "But we, too, can harm you. We cannot come all the way to you in the United States, but individual Arabs may reach you." Iraq had sheltered Arab terrorists, so this wasn't viewed as an idle threat.

U.S. soldiers face off in the desert waiting for the approaching Iraqi army.

As a result, security was tightened throughout the Western world. Government officials were more closely guarded. Even the average person could see the difference. In the United States, a businessman drove his car into an airport parking area. He soon had airport security personnel searching through his car. They even went through a bag of practice golf balls in the car trunk.

However, there were no serious terrorist attacks during Operation Desert Shield.

But Saddam did use the Scuds. Iraq fired the 40-foot long missiles at Israel. Primary targets were the cities of Tel Aviv and Haifa. There were several casualties.

The big question was whether or not Israel would fight back. The United States did not want Israel to strike out against Iraq. The U.S. feared this would weaken the anti-Iraq coalition. Syria and Egypt, in particular, might want out.

So the U.S. very quickly sent Patriot missiles to Israel. The 17-foot long Patriot was an anti-missile missile. It was part of the new military technology. Each Patriot cost $600,000. The Patriot had never been used in combat. The U.S. also sent launchers and crews to operate the weapons.

U.S. Secretary of State James Baker and Prime Minister Shamir of Israel.

For fear of chemical attack by Iraq, U.S. soldiers wear gas masks and protective gear.

Never before had American soldiers defended Israeli soil in a conflict.

The Patriots worked as designed. They were launched from trailers against incoming Scuds. The Patriots exploded into shrapnel when near their targets. Most of the time they brought down the Scuds. The Israeli military did not attack Iraq.

Iraqi Scuds also were fired into Saudi Arabia. Again, Patriots were used to stop them.

There also was the scare of chemical warfare and poison gas attacks. Iraq has used both before. The Israelis feared the Iraqi-fired Scuds might contain chemicals or poison. So Israel issued over four-and-a-half million gas masks. People put on the gas masks whenever there was a Scud attack alert. American forces in Saudi Arabia also were issued gas masks and protective clothing. But there were no chemical or gas attacks during Operation Desert Storm.

Meanwhile in Kuwait, the Iraqi soldiers were terrifying the Kuwaitis. Many died. Women were assaulted. Reports said that the invading soldiers ate the animals in a zoo.

Iraq also held some Westerners as hostages. When Kuwait was invaded, hundreds of thousands of foreign citizens, including Americans, were trapped in Kuwait and Iraq. Most were guest workers from India and the Philippines. Many people fled across the desert to safer havens. Some who didn't escape were used as pawns by Saddam Hussein. He placed them at sites likely to be hit if the coalition began to attack Kuwait or Iraq.

By September 1, 1990, 56 Americans and 137 Britains were being held hostage. Eventually, all Westerners who wished to leave were freed.

American troops keep a persistent eye on the border of Kuwait.

American troops, on guard, fall in for the night.

THE CONFLICT HEATS UP

Through late 1990, the campaign to drive Iraq from Kuwait heated up. "Iraq will not be permitted to annex Kuwait," President Bush said in September. "That's not a threat, not a boast. That's just the way it's going to be."

President Bush had compared Saddam Hussein to Germany's Adolf Hitler, the Nazi dictator during World War II. "A half century ago, our nation and the world paid dearly for appeasing an aggressor who should, and could, have been stopped," Bush said. "We are not going to make the same mistake again."

By fall 1990, the stakes in the gulf confrontation increased. President Bush called up reservists and by mid-October there were 200,000 U.S. forces in the gulf. Just after the November elections in the United States, the president said he was sending up to 200,000 more troops to Saudi Arabia. This would nearly double the U.S. forces in the gulf region. The president actually had made the decision before the elections, but held off announcing it until after the voting.

At Thanksgiving, President Bush went to Saudi Arabia himself for a firsthand look. A few days later, the U.N. Security Council gave its okay to use force after January 15, 1991.

President Bush offered to send Secretary of State Baker to Iraq's capital for "one last talk." He said that would be "going the extra mile." But Saddam Hussein said he couldn't see Baker until only three days before the U.N. deadline.

So the president sent Baker to Geneva, Switzerland, for a meeting with the Iraqi foreign minister. The January 9 meeting between Baker and Tariq Aziz was fruitless.

CONGRESS SAYS GO

Three days later, on January 12, 1991, President Bush received Congress' authorization to go to war in the Gulf. The Senate approved the use of military force 52-47. The House approval was by a margin of 250-183.

House Speaker Thomas Foley, a Democrat from the state of Washington, called the votes "the practical equivalent" of a declaration of war. The president said the vote showed "the U.S. commitment to enforce a complete Iraqi withdrawal (from Kuwait)." The voting followed three days of intense debate.

A MILLION SOLDIERS FACE OFF

As January 1991 began, Iraq had moved an estimated 545,000 armed forces into fighting position. Therefore, there were now over one million armed forces lined up in the Kuwait theater of war. Only some 1.8 million people had lived in Kuwait before it was invaded.

Once Congress authorized military force in the gulf, President Bush said fighting may begin "sooner rather than later" if Iraq did not rapidly withdraw from Kuwait. He said January 15 was "a very real deadline." So the world waited.

On January 5, President Bush issued another warning. It was contained in an undelivered letter intended for Saddam Hussein. Unless Iraq withdrew "from Kuwait completely and without condition," the letter said, "you will lose more than Kuwait."

Saddam was saying that if war came, American forces would "swim in their own blood."

"Everything had to lead to the point where there was no choice but war if Saddam refused to back down, said one commentator.

As the days ticked down to the January 15 deadline set by the United Nations, the world watched with fear and fascination to see if there would be a major war.

On January 16 the fighting began. Operation Desert Shield became Operation Desert Storm.

GLOSSARY

Hafez Assad — President of Syria

Fahd ibn Abdul Aziz — King of Saudi Arabia

Tario Aziz — Foreign Minister of Iraq

James Baker — United States Secretary of State

George Bush — President of the United States

Dick Cheney — United States Secretary of Defense

Marlin Fitzwater — White House Press Secretary

Thomas Foley — Speaker of the United States House of Representatives

Saddam Hussein — President of Iraq

Hosni Mubarek — President of Egypt

General Colin Powell — Chairman of the United States Joint Chiefs of Staff

General H. Norman Schwarzkopf III — United States Army/Field Commander for Operations Desert Shield/Storm

Sheikh Jaber al Ahmad al Sabah — Emir of Kuwait

Eduard Shevardnadze — Soviet Foreign Minister

Lieutenant General Khalid bin Sultan — Saudi Arabian prince/Commander of Pan-Arab Force in Operations Desert Shield/Storm

Margaret Thatcher — British Prime Minister